DRUGS the facts about
ANTIDEPRESSANTS

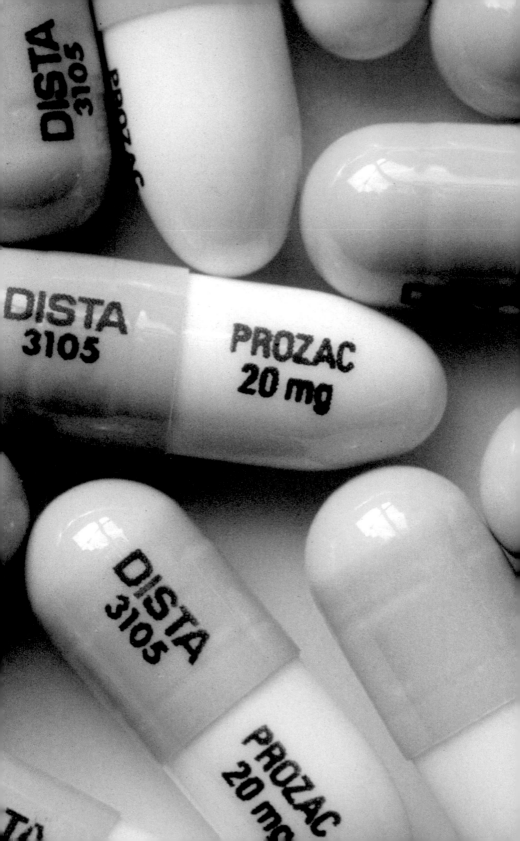

DRUGS the facts about

ANTIDEPRESSANTS

Suzanne LeVert

 **Marshall Cavendish**
Benchmark
New York

Acknowledgment:
Thanks to John Roll, Ph.D., director of Behavioral Pharmacology at UCLA Integrated Substance
Abuse Programs, for his expert review of this manuscript.

Marshall Cavendish Benchmark
99 White Plains Road
Tarrytown, NY 10591
www.marshallcavendish.us

All Internet sites were available and accurate when sent to press.
Library of Congress Cataloging-in-Publication Data

LeVert, Suzanne.
The facts about antidepressants / by Suzanne LeVert.
p. cm.—(Drugs)

Summary: "Describes the history, characteristics, legal status, and abuse of
antidepressants"—Provided by publisher.
Includes bibliographical references and index.
ISBN-13: 978-0-7614-2241-9
ISBN-10: 0-7614-2241-2
1. Antidepressants—Juvenile literature. I. Title. II. Series: Drugs (Benchmark Books (Firm)

RM332.L48 2006
615'.78—dc22
2006002403

Photo Research by Joan Meisel

Cover photo: Scott Camazine./Alamy

The photographs in this book are used by the courtesy of:
Alamy: 1, 2-3, 5, 31, Phototake Inc.; 62, K-Photos;   AP Wide World: 6;
Corbis: 13, Louie Psihoyos; 19, 77, Images.com; Peter Arnold, Inc.: 41,
John Powell; 80, Hans Joachim/Bilderberg; 93, Grames/Bilderberg; 95,
Bilderberg; Photo Researchers, Inc.: 24, 50, John Bavosi, 44, AJ Photo;
66, Will & Deni McIntyre; 86, LADA

Printed in China
1 3 5 6 4 2

CONTENTS

SOME ANTIDEPRESSANT USE IN TEENAGERS HAS BEEN LINKED TO SUICIDE. TERI WILLIAMS, LEFT, AND RHONDA THROWER, RIGHT, BOTH OF ALABAMA, WAIT IN LINE TO SPEAK. THE U.S. FOOD AND DRUG ADMINISTRATION HELD A PUBLIC HEARING ON POSSIBLE SUICIDES IN CLINICAL TRIALS OF ANTIDEPRESSANTS IN KIDS IN BETHESDA, MARYLAND, FEBRUARY 2, 2004. WILLIAMS'S SON COMMITTED SUICIDE AT AGE FOURTEEN WHILE ON ANTIDEPRESSANTS.

1 The Antidepressant Paradox: Cure or Problem?

Antidepressants—drugs used to treat depres-sion and related disorders—are now among the most widely prescribed drugs in the United States, with almost 200 million prescriptions written each year. In recent years, more and more children and adolescents are taking these drugs than ever before. According to statistics gathered by the federal Food and Drug Administration (FDA), physicians wrote more than 15 million prescriptions for antidepressants for children and teens in 2003.

Studies of the effects of these drugs on this population, however, have raised concerns among doctors and parents. In 2003, studies performed in Great Britain showed that the risk of suicide increased among teens taking certain antidepressants. Another study that year performed in Canada found that antidepressant medication did little to alleviate symptoms of depression in teens as compared with a placebo. Taken together, this data prompted the U.S. Food and Drug Administration (FDA) in 2004 to mandate drug manufacturers to put label warnings on antidepressants to warn doctors and patients of the risk of suicide in teens. Since that time, prescriptions for antidepressants for teens have dropped some 20 percent.

Despite the controversy over the use of antidepressants for children and teenagers, there is little question that this medication serves a useful purpose in treating the very serious, sometimes deadly, disorder of depression. The latest statistics about teens and depression are daunting: According to a study published in the December 2005 issue of *Journal of Adolescent Health*, the number of visits associated with adolescent depression from 1995 to 2002 more than doubled, from 1.4 million visits in 1995 to 3.2 million in 2002.

According to a report issued by the Substance Abuse and Mental Health Services Administration (SAMHSA) in 2005, about 14 percent of adolescents (people twelve to seventeen years of age) will experience major depression at some point during their teen years. Nearly one in ten American teenagers, or 2.2 million, experienced major depression in 2004. About 12 percent of youth aged sixteen or seventeen faced severe depression in 2004, compared with about 5 percent of those twelve or thirteen years old. Among those age fourteen or fifteen, 9 percent experienced a major episode.

In addition to the debilitating symptoms of depression, including weight loss, withdrawal from social activities, and poor school performance, teens with depression are more likely than other teens to attempt or commit suicide. Every year, about 5,000 teenagers, most of them depressed, commit suicide and another 500,000 attempt suicide. According to the American Psychiatric Association, more than half of all teens who suffer from depression will attempt suicide at least once and about 7 percent of that number will die as a result. Statistics collected by the Centers for Disease Control reveal that suicide is the third leading cause of death (after car accidents and homicide) among young people aged ten to twenty-four years, accounting for 11.7 percent of all deaths in this age group.

And that is the paradox facing physicians, parents, and teen patients. Is it riskier for depressed teens to take antidepressants that might trigger suicidal thoughts or riskier to treat the condition with talk therapy alone? The most recent study of antidepressant use among teens shows that the benefits of taking the drugs appear to outweigh the risks they pose of suicide for most people. In a report published in the February 2005 issue of *Nature Reviews Drug Discovery*, researchers reviewed studies in which blood samples from suicide victims were screened. They found that fewer than 20 percent of those samples showed evidence of recent antidepressant use. University of California at Los Angeles professor of psychiatry Julio Licinio, who conducted the study, told a reporter that "Our findings strongly suggest that these individuals who committed suicide were not reacting to their [medication]. They actually killed themselves due to untreated depression. This was especially true in men and in people under thirty."

The American Psychiatric Society, among other mainstream medical organizations, has long recommended a combination of psychotherapy and counseling and drug treatment. Psychotherapy can help uncover some of the underlying causes or triggers of the depressive episode as well as help depressed teens better cope with their lives and their condition. Furthermore, coupling psychotherapy with drug treatment allows physicians to monitor patients more closely and on a more regular basis. However, according to the December 2005 study in the *Journal of Adolescent Health*, depressed adolescents were more likely to be treated with antidepressants alone rather than with a combination of psychotherapy and medication.

Understanding antidepressants and how they work to alleviate depression, as well as learning what side effects they cause, is an ongoing process in the medical profession. Weighing the risks and benefits of giving antidepressants to teenagers with depression, rather than choosing psychotherapy alone or leaving the disease untreated, remains a matter to be decided by doctors and parents.

Although antidepressants most often are used to alleviate depression, it should be noted that doctors may prescribe the drugs to treat other mood disorders, including anxiety, eating disorders, and even to help people to quit smoking. In addition, many teens who are depressed also suffer from other conditions, such as attention deficit/hyperactivity disorder (ADHD), and substance abuse that may require treatment with other medications. That's another reason teens may require especially close monitoring by a physician as they cope with their emotional and physical health problems.

What Is Depression?
Defining depression is not an easy task because the condition tends to affect everyone in a slightly different way. In fact, it may be easier to describe what depression is *not* rather than what it is. It isn't "the blues" or feeling low for a few hours or even for several days. It isn't the sadness that comes after a relationship breaks up or the drop in self-esteem that occurs after failing an exam or losing a sports tournament. Depression is not grief. It isn't a bad mood or feeling grouchy.

Instead, depression is a whole body illness, involving changes in body chemistry that cause a variety of symptoms. Depression affects not just the emotions but also physical health and thought and behavior patterns. One of the reasons that depres-

sion so often goes undiagnosed—especially in teens—
is that some people remain unaware that their physical problems could be related to a mood disorder.

There are three primary categories of depression
among teens and adults: major depression,
dysthymia, and bipolar disorder. Major depression is
a disorder characterized by one or more episodes
that significantly alter behavior and health, often
interfering with the ability to manage daily life.
These episodes consist of at least two weeks of
depressed mood or loss of interest plus five of nine
other symptoms of depression, including weight loss,
disturbances in motor control, and an inability to
concentrate, among others. In its most severe form, it
may require hospitalization for a period of time.

Dysthymia, or chronic mild depression, tends to
have milder symptoms but also can be longer lasting. Teenagers are diagnosed with dysthymia when
they have experienced a depressed mood for at
least one year (two years for adults) along with low
energy, poor appetite, lack of concentration, and
feelings of hopelessness, among other symptoms.
Whether or not dysthymia is a separate entity from
major depression or simply a less intense version of
the same disorder remains a subject of debate.

Several other subcategories of depression exist,
each with its own set of symptoms and triggers:

- *Seasonal affective disorder (SAD)* involves
  periods of depression on an annual basis
  during the same time each year, beginning
  most often between the months of

October and November as the days grow shorter and ending in March or April with the coming of spring. It is estimated that from 4 percent to 6 percent of the population suffers with SAD, most of them in the northern part of the country where it stays darker longer. Many experts believe that lack of light triggers biochemical changes in the brain that contribute to the development of depression.

- *Premenstrual dysphoric disorder (PMDD)* is related to premenstrual syndrome. PMDD occurs in an estimated 3 percent of all menstruating women, including teenagers,

SOME PEOPLE SUFFER FROM DEPRESSION CAUSED BY A LACK OF SUNLIGHT. HERE, A PATIENT RECEIVES LIGHT THERAPY, WHICH IS THOUGHT TO HELP TREAT SEASONAL DEPRESSION.

who experience symptoms of depression during the last week of their menstrual cycles and cannot function as usual at work, home, or school.

• *Bipolar disorder*. Bipolar disorder, also called manic-depressive illness, affects about 2.3 million American adults, or about 1 percent of the population. Most cases of bipolar disorder first arise during adolescence. The symptoms of bipolar disorder vary greatly from person to person, but involve periods of depressive symptoms such as sadness and low energy followed by manic phases that often involve feelings of intense elation and self-confidence and behavior that may involve taking more physical, sexual, and emotional risks than usual.

The Symptoms of Depression

Depression feels different to every person who experiences it. There are, however, a wide variety of common symptoms that together define depression, and they involve our emotions, thought processes, behavior, and physical health.

Although we think of depression as a mental illness, it also has many somatic, or physical, symptoms, including headaches, stomach problems, insomnia, and loss of appetite. In fact, most people with depression first visit a doctor complaining not of emotional problems but of physical ones. Another physical symptom is fatigue, a lack of energy and motivation that can be overwhelming. In other cases, depressed teens and adults report feeling more agitated and irritable than usual, pacing and fidgeting rather than feeling lethargic. Another common symptom is gastrointestinal distress, especially irritable bowel syndrome. Changes in eating habits also occur in severe depression. In most cases, depressed people lose their appetite and hence begin to lose weight.

Perhaps the most obvious impact depression makes is on our feelings and moods. Sadness is the most common feeling. Among young women, tearfulness is its most frequent expression; young men with the disorder tend to withdraw. But sadness is just one aspect of depression's emotional spectrum. The disorder can trigger a host of other feelings including:

- *Emptiness.* Teens with depression feel empty and unconnected to the world. Nothing gives them pleasure, not even favorite activities or beloved friends.
- *Hopelessness.* One reason so few teens suffering from depression reach out for help is that they truly believe that nothing could change their mood or situation. The present is unbearable and, in their minds, the future can only get worse.

Symptoms of Depression in Teens

Symptoms of child and adolescent depression vary in severity and duration and may be different from those in adults. Diagnosing depression in these age groups can be difficult because early symptoms can be hard to detect or may be attributed to other causes. Among the signs of depression in children and teens include:

- Missed school or poor school performance;
- Changes in eating and sleeping habits;
- Withdrawal from friends and activities once enjoyed;
- Persistent sadness and hopelessness;
- Problems with authority;
- Indecision, lack of concentration, or forgetfulness;
- Poor self-esteem or guilt;
- Overreaction to criticism;
- Frequent physical complaints, such as headaches and stomachaches;
- Anger and rage;
- Lack of enthusiasm, low energy, or motivation;
- Drug and/or alcohol abuse;
- Thoughts of death or suicide.

- *Remorse.* If the future looks bleak to a depressed person, the past is a place filled with disappointment, darkness, and regret.
- *Guilt.* Sometimes depression brings on a debilitating cycle of diminished activity and withdrawal followed by anxiety and then guilt. Lacking energy and motivation, many depressed people fail to perform regular chores, fall behind at school, and neglect the people closest to them. This creates tension and stress, more reasons to feel like an unworthy failure.

When it comes to bipolar disorder, periods of depression are followed by periods of mania. Symptoms of bipolar depression are similar to those experienced by people who suffer only from depression (e.g., despair, hopelessness, lethargy, changes in sleep patterns, and appetite). The symptoms of mania include severe changes in mood, either becoming unusually happy or silly or very irritable, angry, agitated, or aggressive. Other symptoms include:

- unrealistic highs in self-esteem; for example, a teenager who feels all-powerful or like a superhero with special powers;
- great increase in energy and the ability to go with little or no sleep for days without feeling tired;
- increase in talking—the adolescent talks too much, too fast, changes topics too quickly, and cannot be interrupted;

17

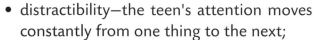

- distractibility—the teen's attention moves constantly from one thing to the next;
- repeated high risk-taking behavior, such as abusing alcohol and drugs, reckless driving, or sexual promiscuity.

Who Gets Depressed?

Depression does not discriminate: The disorder affects people of every age, religion, race, and culture. Although each one of us has a specific set of genetic, social, and personal qualities that puts us at greater or lesser risk of becoming depressed, there are some general categories of people who appear to be at significantly higher risk than the average population. Among the factors that raise the risk are:

- **Family history**. Like many other physical and psychological disorders, depression often runs in families. Although researchers have not yet identified the specific genes involved, studies show that relatives of people who have depression have an overall two to three times higher risk of developing the disease than people without a family history. A child with one depressed parent has a 26 percent higher risk than the rest of the population; with two depressed parents, the risk increases to about 46 percent.
- **Age**. Depression recognizes no age barrier. Young children, teenagers, and men and

SOME PEOPLE SUFFER FROM BIPOLAR DISORDER, WHICH IS MARKED BY PERIODS OF DEPRESSION CYCLING WITH PERIODS OF MANIA.

women of all ages develop depression. The most vulnerable age for depression in both men and women is between the ages of twenty-four and forty-four. But children and adolescents are also at risk. About 1 percent of young children develop the disorder and that number sharply increases during and following puberty. More than 10 percent—some studies say as many as 25 percent—of adolescents suffer from depression at some point during their teen years. In addition, depression is often masked and/or complicated by other conditions in teens, from learning disabilities to eating disorders to substance abuse. And depression in this age group can be especially lethal if left untreated. More than 4,200 adolescents kill themselves in the United States each year and another 400,000 make unsuccessful attempts. In fact, suicide is the third leading cause of death for teenagers in the United States, after car accidents and homicide.

- **Gender**. At every age group except early childhood when boys and girls are equally likely to become depressed, females are two to three times more likely than males to develop major depression and other depressive disorders. In the SAMSHA study, 13.1 percent of young women ages ten to twenty-four reported being depressed in 2004 as compared with 5 percent of young men.

Why Do Teens Get Depressed?

Brown University reported in its *Child and Adolescent Behavior Letter* in April 2002 that many parents simply do not recognize the symptoms of depression in their adolescent children. They found that even parents who have good communication with their children do not necessarily realize it when a child is depressed. One reason for this lack of recognition is that so many adults forget how difficult and fraught with stress and emotional turmoil adolescence can be. Indeed, experts suggest that up to half of all adolescents with depression remain untreated because no one recognizes their symptoms.

Depression is a biochemical disorder involving an imbalance of brain chemicals called neurotransmitters. The drugs used to treat this condition act to restore balance to the brain. What triggers the imbalance to occur in the first place is largely unknown and definitely varies from individual to individual. Some of the reasons that some teens may become depressed include the following:

- **Significant events** such as the death of a loved one, parents' divorce, moving to a new area, or breaking up with a girlfriend or boyfriend can prompt symptoms. Adolescent depression can occur from neglect, the prolonged absence of someone who is a source of care and nurturance, abuse and bullying, damage to self-esteem, or too many life changes occurring too quickly. In some teenagers, any major change may provoke depression.

- **Earlier traumatic experiences** such as abuse or incest often emerge and cause great distress as the child becomes a teen. As a young child, the victim did not have the life experience or language to process these painful experiences or to protect himself or herself. Feelings of pain, depression, and powerlessness result as memories emerge in adolescence.
- **Stress**, especially if the adolescent lacks emotional support.
- **Hormonal/physical changes** that occur during puberty also cause new and unexpected emotions. They also may cause a chemical disturbance in the brain that can lead to a major depressive episode.
- **Medical conditions** such as hypothyroidism can affect hormone balance and mood. Chronic physical illness also can cause depression. When a medical condition is diagnosed and treated by a doctor, the depression usually disappears.
- **Substance abuse** can cause changes in brain chemistry.
- **Allergies** to foods such as wheat, sugar, and milk cause or exacerbate symptoms of depression.

- **Nutritional deficiencies** may be caused by an amino acid imbalance or vitamin deficiency.
- **Genetics** can predispose a teen to depression if the illness runs in the family.

No matter what triggers depression in teens, the resulting symptoms are painful and often intractable. In addition to suicide, depressed adolescents are at high risk for school failure, social isolation, promiscuity, and "self-medication" with drugs or alcohol if their condition is left untreated. Furthermore, some studies indicate that depression in adolescent brains, which are growing and changing at a rapid rate, may cause permanent changes in neuronal connections. These changes may leave teens more susceptible to future episodes of depression and other mood disorders, underscoring the importance of getting effective treatment as soon as possible.

THE HIGHLY COMPLEX LIMBIC SYSTEM OF THE BRAIN IS CONSIDERED THE SEAT OF THE EMOTIONS.

2 The Biology and Treatment of Depression

Do you feel sad, hopeless, or empty every day?

Do activities that once gave you pleasure no longer interest you?

Have you lost or gained weight without trying?

Do you seem to act and think more slowly or quickly than you have in the past?

Are you tired or lacking in energy?

Do you feel ill, as if something is wrong with you?

Do you think of yourself as worthless?

Do you feel very guilty about your past or present behavior?

Do you have recurrent thoughts about death or suicide?

Are you unable to function as you once did, with your friends and family, or at school?

These questions are among those that health professionals may ask a young person whom they suspect may be suffering from depression. They help both patients and doctors more accurately identify feelings and emotions that people with depression typically experience. Later in this chapter, the other diagnostic tools used by physicians are outlined. In the meantime, it's important to realize how the body and brain create and experience emotions and moods. That way, you'll be able to understand how antidepressants work and why their effects and side effects occur.

The Biology and Pathology of Depression
Medical researchers have dubbed the brain "medicine's last frontier." Indeed, it wasn't until the 1990s that scientists learned a full 90 percent of what they now know about brain anatomy and physiology. What they discovered is that the "mind" (thoughts, emotions, moods, and memories) and the "brain" (tissues, chemicals, and nerve cells) are not separate entities but instead intimately intertwined. Mental experiences affect the way the brain functions and brain processes affect the way we think, feel, and behave. This understanding has led to more effective treatment for mental disorders, since it recognized both their biological and psychological aspects.

The human brain and nervous system form a vast communications network. Every emotion we feel, action we take, and physiological function we undergo is processed through the brain and the nerve fibers that extend down the spinal cord and throughout the body.

The brain itself is divided into several large regions, each of which is responsible for certain activities. The brain stem, a primitive structure at the base of the skull, controls basic physiological functions such as heart rate and respiration. The cerebral cortex is the largest and most highly developed portion of the brain. Divided into four lobes, the cortex is the center of the brain's higher powers where the activities we define as "thinking"—thought, perception, memory, and communication—take place.

On top of the brain stem and buried under the cortex is another set of structures called the limbic system. Scientists believe that this highly complex, and still largely unmapped, region is "home base" to our emotions. It receives and regulates emotional information and helps to govern sexual desire, appetite, and stress. Four main centers of the limbic system are the thalamus, hypothalamus, the hippocampus, and the amygdala. Together, the thalamus and hypothalamus form a kind of "brain within the brain," regulating a variety of human processes, including appetite, thirst, sleep, and certain aspects of mood and behavior. The hippocampus and amygdala help to create memory as well as to gauge emotions.

Thanks to the remarkable advances made in medical technology, scientists have been able to trace how the limbic system registers emotion and then produces emotional reactions in cooperation with other parts of the brain and body. Studies performed at the National Institute of Mental Health during the mid–1990s showed that emotional opposites like happiness and sadness involve quite independent patterns of activity. When we feel happy, activity in the region of the cerebral cortex responsible for forethought and planning decreases dramatically, as does activity in the amygdala. When we're unhappy, on the other hand, the amygdala and another part of the cortex become more active. The division of the labor within the brain may be why we're able to experience a seemingly contradictory feeling like "bittersweetness." Take a high school athlete who plays on the track team. When she loses her event, but the team wins as a whole, she is both disappointed in her performance and thrilled at the team's victory.

When it comes to depression, studies show something else quite interesting. It seems that the same area of the brain—the left prefrontal cortex—appears to be involved in both depression and ordinary sadness, but in different ways. It becomes more active during ordinary sadness, but almost completely shuts down with depression. That may explain the emptiness and numbness many depressed people report. Another finding is that the hippocampal regions of depressed patients are actually smaller than those in normal patients because depression somehow prevents new neurons in this region from forming as usual.

Mapping the Synapse

Each nerve cell, or neuron, contains three important parts: the central body, the dendrites, and the axon. Messages from other nerve cells enter the cell body through the dendrites, which are branchlike projections extending from the cell body. Once the central cell body processes the messages, it can then pass the information to its neighboring neuron through a cablelike fiber called the axon. At speeds faster than you can imagine, information about every aspect of human physiology, emotion, and thought zips through the body from one neuron to another in precisely this manner.

But there's a hitch: The axon of one neuron does not attach directly to its neighboring nerve cell. Instead, a tiny gap separates the terminal of one axon from the dendrites of the neuron with which it seeks to communicate. This gap is called a synapse. For a message to make it across a synapse, it requires the help of neurotransmitters, chemicals stored in packets at the end of each nerve cell. When a cell is ready to send a message, its axon releases a certain amount and type of neurotransmitter. This chemical then diffuses across the synapse to bind to special molecules, called receptors, that sit on the surface of the dendrites of the adjacent nerve cell.

When a neurotransmitter couples to a receptor, it acts like a key fitting into a starter that triggers a biochemical process in that neuron. The receptor molecules link up with other molecules in the cell body, completing the transmission of the message. Whenever this occurs, whatever amount of neurotransmitter remains in the synapse is either destroyed or, in the process called "reuptake," sucked back into the nerve cell that released it.

Scientists have identified forty to fifty neurotransmitters and believe at least fifty more are yet to be identified. Each must be present in sufficient amounts for the brain and nervous system to function properly. When too much or too little neurotransmitter exists, or if the cells are unable to use the chemicals properly, mental and physical disturbances may occur. Indeed, biochemical balance appears to be an important key to mental health.

The Brain and Depression
In most cases of mental illness, certain neurotransmitters are not present in the right amounts or are not used efficiently. When it comes to depression in adults and teenagers, an imbalance of three neurotransmitters—serotonin, dopamine, and norepinephrine—appears to be involved. These same chemical imbalances also occur, to greater and lesser degrees, in teens who suffer from anxiety, eating disorders, obsessive-compulsive disorder, and several other psychological disturbances.

Among those three neurotransmitters, serotonin appears to play the largest role in depression. With the most extensive network of any neurotransmitter, serotonin influences a wide range of brain activities, including mood, behavior, movement, pain, sexual activity, appetite, hormone secretion, and heart rate. People with depression have been found to have lower amounts than usual of serotonin in the brain, as have people suffering from eating disorders.

Another important neurotransmitter is dopamine, which follows two main pathways in the brain. One pathway connects to a portion of the brain

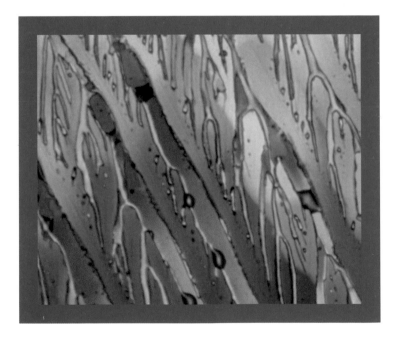

THIS PHOTOMICROGRAPH SHOWS DOPAMINE. DEPRESSION CAN RESULT IF A PERSON DOES NOT PRODUCE ENOUGH DOPAMINE.

called the corpus striatum, which controls movement. When this pathway malfunctions, as it does in diseases such as Parkinson's and Huntington's chorea, problems with muscle control arise. The other dopamine pathway extends into the limbic system. When dopamine does not exist in proper amounts or is unable to reach organs of the limbic system, emotional problems such as depression may occur.

Norepinephrine is the third neurotransmitter thought to be involved in depression. Lower than normal amounts of this chemical have been measured in people who are depressed, as well as in people suffering with the eating disorder called anorexia. Scientists have found a few different medications that help restore proper norepinephrine levels to the brain.

Like serotonin, norepinephrine molecules contain only one of a certain kind of protein, called an amine, so it is classified as a monoamine. One class of drugs developed to alleviate depression concentrates on preventing a substance called monoamine oxidase from breaking down monoamines like norepinephrine and serotonin. When medication (called monoamine oxidase inhibitors, or MAOIs) stops the action of this substance, more norepinephrine and serotonin are available to nerve cells, allowing cells to send and receive the right signals. Tricyclic antidepressants also work on restoring norepinephrine and serotonin activity.

As medical technology, such as magnetic resonance imagery (MRI) and other diagnostic techniques continue to improve, scientists will learn even more about these neurotransmitters and how they affect emotion, thought, and behavior. In the meantime, they've already discovered that neuro-transmitters do not work alone in transmitting messages, but instead cooperate directly with another system of the body: the endocrine system, which produces chemicals called hormones.

The Endocrine Connection
What lets your brain "know" that your stomach is empty and makes you feel hungry? What causes you to feel sleepy at night? Why does your heart beat faster when something frightens or excites you?

The answer to all of these questions is the same: Hormones, chemicals produced by the glands of the endocrine system, trigger the onset and termina-tion of these and other actions and reactions. They work with neurotransmitters as messengers, send-ing information and instructions to organs and cells throughout the body. In fact, several chemicals are both neurotransmitters and hormones, depending on where they work and what messages they are meant to transmit. Norepinephrine, for instance, acts as a neurotransmitter in the brain, while it per-forms as a hormone on the heart and blood vessels during times of stress.

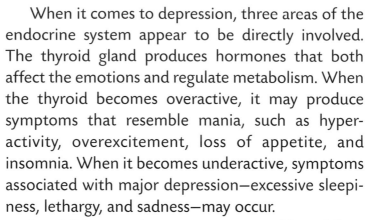

When it comes to depression, three areas of the endocrine system appear to be directly involved. The thyroid gland produces hormones that both affect the emotions and regulate metabolism. When the thyroid becomes overactive, it may produce symptoms that resemble mania, such as hyperactivity, overexcitement, loss of appetite, and insomnia. When it becomes underactive, symptoms associated with major depression—excessive sleepiness, lethargy, and sadness—may occur.

In addition, sex hormones start to ebb and flow in both girls and boys as they enter puberty. Since the endocrine system works as a unit, with the level of one hormone influencing the levels of all others, the activity of sex hormones has a profound effect on far more than the reproductive system. The higher risk of mood swings and depression experienced by teens may well be related to the surge in sex hormones during this period.

A third important endocrine connection to depression is called the HPA axis because it involves the hypothalamus, pituitary, and adrenal glands. The HPA axis is involved in the regulation of cortisol, a steroid hormone secreted during prolonged stress as well as at regular intervals throughout the day. Whenever the brain senses danger or difficulty, it responds by sending chemical signals that prepare the body either to fight or flee the impending situation. Called the "fight or flight" response, this reaction involves the release of cortisol from the adrenal glands. Cortisol then converts norepinephrine into epinephrine, or adrenalin, making the heart pump harder; the muscles tense for action; the sweat glands open; and the mind quickens.

Scientists studying depression discovered that a larger percentage of depressed people have a much higher level of cortisol in their bloodstreams than normal. Strangely enough, although depression usually causes a decrease in feelings of agitation and activity (just the sort of biological state cortisol triggers), cortisol levels in depressed people are even higher than in people with disorders more commonly associated with extreme stress, such as anxiety and psychosis.

What causes cortisol levels to be so high in depression is still under investigation. It may be related to the balance of the body's internal rhythms, which are studied in a science known as chronobiology. Cortisol is one of the many hormones the body produces on a relatively automatic, time-released basis. Some researchers believe that, with depression, the internal rhythms of hormone production may become irregular and out of sync, causing a host of physiological and emotional symptoms. Another theory proposes that depression somehow causes the HPA axis to malfunction so that the body is unable to stop cortisol production after stress has passed. Suffering from prolonged stress—as many teens do in today's highly competitive and ever-changing world—may be a triggering factor for depression in many individuals.

Body Rhythms Out of Sync

Far more than we realize, our internal and external lives are regulated by rhythms of light and dark, of sleep and wakefulness, of fluctuating body temperature, blood pressure, and hormone secretion. Researchers believe that our rhythms are driven by two different oscillators: One is very consistent and controls body temperature and many hormonal secretions. The other is more fluid and subject to change, and controls sleep/wake and activity/rest patterns. Chronobiologists think that it is when these two oscillators become desynchronized that illness—mental or physical—occurs.

What sets up these physiological cycles and keeps them on schedule? There are many different *zeitgebers* (as the term is known in German); or "time-givers," that establish our body clocks. Some *zeitgebers* are internal, set up and maintained regardless of external factors. Others depend heavily on cues we receive from the outside world: the knowledge we have of time established by clocks and watches (how often have we suddenly felt hungry only when we noticed it's "lunchtime"), the smell of coffee brewing in the morning, the sound of traffic picking up during rush hour in the afternoon.

Perhaps the strongest and best known *zeitgeber* is the rising and setting of the sun: The light it brings each morning and takes away at dusk causes the release or inactivation of certain hormones that trigger our mood and behavior. For example, we don't go to sleep when it's dark only out of habit, or because darkness makes activity more difficult, or even just because we're tired. It's largely because the body produces a hormone called melatonin when the eyes tell the brain that it is dark.

Once produced, melatonin then signals to the rest of the body that it is time to rest. When the sun comes up, the body stops producing melatonin, which triggers the release of more action-oriented hormones, such as cortisol. Our body temperature and blood pressure begin to rise, revving the body up for daytime activity.

Chronobiology has a number of different effects on our health. The sense of hearing, taste, and smell, for instance, tend to be most acute in the middle of the night—around 3 a.m.—then fall off during the morning, then rise again to a new high between 5 p.m. and 7 p.m., which may be one of the reasons why the evening meal tends to be more sumptuous than breakfast or lunch. Pain tolerance is highest in the afternoon. Asthma attacks are more likely to take place in the early morning when lung function is at a daily low.

Chronobiology also explores the effect rhythms have on mental health, including their influence on depression. It seems logical to assume there's a connection, that sleeping difficulties, changes in appetite and eating habits and poor concentration are related to regular rhythms of life. Some of these rhythms are circadian in nature, which means that they occur in cycles of roughly twenty-four hours. Blood pressure, heart rate, the sleep/wake cycle, appetite, some aspects of sleep itself, and body temperature are just a few examples of circadian rhythms.

Recent studies show that circadian rhythms in depressed people are significantly off-kilter when compared with the daily rhythms of healthy individuals. Normal nighttime increases in melatonin secretion are absent in three of four depressed people studied. One reason for this disruption is that melatonin is derived from the neurotransmitter serotonin, which also becomes imbalanced in most people with depression.

Sleep is what most suffers from the melatonin imbalance, with most depressed people sleeping much more or much less than usual. In addition, the pattern of sleep itself is different. Normally, sleep consists of four stages plus REM (rapid eye movement), the near–waking state during which we dream. These stages occur in repeating ninety-minute cycles throughout the night, with REM occupying as little as ten minutes per cycle at the beginning of sleep, then increasing in length toward morning. With depression, REM sleep occurs far more quickly after the onset of sleep and diminishes toward morning. That means that depressed people experience fewer deep, restorative periods of sleep than people who aren't depressed.

At the same time, a lack of sleep—for any reason—may not only be a symptom of depression, but also a contributing factor in the development of the disorder. In one study presented at the nineteenth Annual Meeting of the Associated Professional Sleep Societies in June 2005, depressed seniors with insomnia were seventeen times more likely to remain depressed after a year than patients who were sleeping well. In a separate study also presented at the June 2005 meeting, seniors with insomnia and no history of depression were six times more likely to experience an episode of depression than seniors without insomnia. Although this research focused on seniors, scientists expressed confidence that the results could apply to anyone who did not receive sufficient sleep on a regular basis.

The link between lack of sleep and depression may be a clue to why rates of depression are so high among teens. Recent studies show that teens are simply not getting enough sleep. During the teen years, the body's rhythms are reset: the body suddenly wants to fall asleep later and wake up later than it did at a younger age. Unlike young children and adults, most teens have a circadian rhythm that triggers sleep to come at a later hour and that continues until later in the morning. This change in the circadian rhythm seems to be due to the fact that melatonin is produced later at night for teens, which can make it harder for teens to fall asleep earlier.

To compound the challenge, these biological changes coincide with a particularly busy personal time for teens. The pressure to do well in school is more intense than when they were younger children, and many teens must study harder in order to achieve. Most teens also have other demands on their time, including sports and extracurricular activities or fitting in a part-time job to save money for college. A recent poll conducted by the National Sleep Foundation found that 60 percent of children under the age of eighteen complained of being tired during the day and 15 percent said they fell asleep at school at some point during the year.

Diagnosing Depression
Unlike the process involved in diagnosing most physical illnesses, no blood, urine, or X-ray tests exist to confirm or rule out depression. Instead, doctors make a diagnosis by interpreting symptoms and comparing them to a standard set of criteria. Most clinicians use the criteria outlined in a text called *The Diagnostic and Statistical Manual of Mental Disorders*. The *DSM-IV* (the IV is because it has been revised four times), as it's commonly known, has been the bible of psychiatric diagnosis since it was first published in 1952. The *DSM-IV* organizes symptoms according to disorder, taking away some—but far from all—of the once arbitrary process of psychiatric diagnosis.

The *DSM-IV* allows the physician to make what is known as a differential diagnosis. By taking an inventory of symptoms—both physical and emotional—and comparing it to the criteria in the manual, he or she can rule out other potential causes and narrow

THIS BOY ON A SKATEBOARD IS GETTING PLENTY OF SUNLIGHT AND EXERCISE, KEYS TO KEEPING ONE'S BODY IN SYNC WITH ONE'S EMOTIONS.

down the diagnosis. It is especially important, and often quite difficult, to discern which of the various depressive disorders, from depression to bipolar disorder to anxiety, may be responsible. When it comes to teens, it is important for doctors to make sure to uncover any coexisting condition, such as ADHD or drug abuse, and treat those symptoms along with the depression.

Symptoms of Major Depression— In Adults and Teens

A doctor may make a diagnosis of major depression if the following is true: five (or more) of the following symptoms have been present during the same two-week period and represent a change from previous functioning; at least one of the symptoms is either depressed mood, or loss of interest or pleasure.

- depressed mood most of the day, nearly every day. In children and adolescents, can be irritable mood
- markedly diminished interest or pleasure in all, or almost all, activities nearly every day
- significant weight loss when not dieting, or weight gain (a change of more than 5 percent of body weight in a month), or decrease or increase in appetite nearly every day
- Insomnia or hypersomnia nearly every day
- psychomotor agitation or retardation nearly every day
- fatigue or loss of energy nearly every day
- feelings of worthlessness or excessive or inappropriate guilt nearly every day
- diminished ability to think or concentrate, or indecisiveness, nearly every day
- recurrent thoughts of death (not just fear of dying), recurrent suicidal ideation without a specific plan, or a suicide attempt, or a specific plan for committing suicide

The first thing a doctor will do is ask a patient to describe all symptoms, both physical and psychological. Taking a medical history of both the patient and the family is also important in order to identify any patterns of illness. The doctor will also perform a complete physical examination, including taking blood and urine samples. This examination will help to rule out any possible underlying physical problems that might cause or exacerbate depressive symptoms. These include:

- Endocrine disorders, particularly thyroid disease and diabetes mellitus;
- Central nervous system diseases, including multiple sclerosis, Alzheimer's disease, and stroke;
- Cancer;
- Heart disease;
- Infectious diseases such as hepatitis, mononucleosis, and tuberculosis.

If the doctor discovers an underlying illness, treatment of that disorder may alleviate the depressive symptoms. However, many chronically ill patients require ongoing talk therapy or treatment with medication in order to recover from the accompanying depression. If no other condition exists, the doctor will work with the patient to come up with a treatment plan that may include medications as well as counseling and other forms of support.

Doctors wrote more than 15 million antidepressant prescriptions for teens in 2005.

3 Antidepressants: An Overview

Treating depression with medication designed to help restore balance among neurotransmitters in the brain has been a staple of medical practice for several decades. Among children and adolescents, however, drug treatment remains controversial largely because studies of young people using this type of medication remain limited. To date, most antidepressant studies have been carried out on adults. Nevertheless, more than 15 million prescriptions for antidepressants were written by physicians for teens in 2005. In this chapter, the many different antidepressants available, how scientists believe they work, and their effects (desired actions) and side effects (unintended consequences) are discussed.

Antidepressants have been prescribed and studied for more than three decades in adults. We know that for the most part these medications are quite safe. Their side effects, which differ from drug to drug and may include dry mouth, restlessness, weight gain or loss, a loss of sexual desire, constipation, and changes in appetite and sleep patterns, are usually mild and tend to subside after a few weeks or months. They work for the vast majority of people, including teenagers, who suffer from depression, alleviating their symptoms and considerably shortening the course of their disease.

It is still unclear exactly how and why these medications work. The intricate workings of the brain and endocrine system remain something of a mystery. Brain chemistry—the production and formation of neurotransmitters—is particularly complex, and it is only in the last few decades that scientists have learned enough about it to design drugs that help to restore any imbalances that occur.

Understanding Antidepressants

Three types of drugs—each of which works to fine-tune the balance of neurotransmitters in a slightly different way—have been found to be most effective in treating depression: selective serotonin reuptake inhibitors (SSRIs), tricyclic antidepressants (TCAs), and monoamine oxidase inhibitors (MAOIs). There are also a number of so-called "second generation" antidepressants that are unrelated to the others but are known to help alleviate depression. These include bupropion (Wellbutrin), trazodone (Desyrel), and venlafaxine (Effexor), with new medications frequently developed.

Finally, people who suffer from bipolar disorder do not take antidepressants at all—in fact, some SSRIs and new generation medications may actually trigger or worsen manic phases of the disorder. The most commonly used drugs are lithium, anticonvulsants, and mood stabilizers. In some cases, once a person's mood has been stabilized, more conventional antidepressants can be used to combat the depressive phase of the disease.

When depression is complicated by other psychological disorders such as anxiety or an eating disorder, as frequently occurs in teens, other drugs may be used alone or in combination with an antidepressant.

In a Stanford University School of Wellness study, selective serotonin reuptake inhibitors (SSRIs) accounted for 76 percent of the antidepressants prescribed to adolescents in 1995, rising slightly to 81 percent in 2002. Although fluoxetine (Prozac) remained the most-prescribed antidepressant, its share of SSRI use shrank as newer drugs came on the market. In 1995, fluoxetine prescriptions accounted for 41 percent of the SSRI prescriptions for adolescents but dropped to 31 percent in 2002.

Which drug or combination of drugs works for any given individual depends largely upon his or her particular brain chemistry and constellation of symp-

Warnings Common to All Antidepressants

Although each type of antidepressant works in a slightly different way and may trigger different side effects, there are certain warnings that anyone who takes antidepressants should heed:

- Do not drink alcohol.
- Avoid taking any other medications—even over-the-counter drugs or herbal remedies—without the express knowledge and permission of a physician.
- Never stop taking antidepressants without first discussing it with a physician.
- Tell the physician if you are pregnant or want to become pregnant.
- Report any thoughts of suicide or death to a physician immediately.

toms. Again, only fluoxetine, or Prozac, is currently approved by the FDA for use in teenagers. Because of the high rates at which doctors prescribe other medications off-label—that means, without FDA approval—to teens, however, it's important to gain an understanding of all types of antidepressants.

Monoamine Oxidase Inhibitors (MAOIs)

Monoamine oxidase inhibitors (MAOIs) were the first type of antidepressant used, dating back to the 1950s. The oldest type of antidepressant, MAOIs are rarely prescribed to treat adolescent depression. Usually, physicians prescribe them only when no other types of medication have worked to alleviate symptoms. They are also more likely to help those with atypical depression—those who gain weight instead of lose it and sleep more than usual instead of less—than those with typical depression.

MAOIs work by blocking the action of monoamine oxidase, which usually works to metabolize, or use up, the neurotransmitters serotonin, dopamine, and norepinephrine after their release into the synapse. By blocking this action, MAOIs allow more of these chemicals to build up inside and outside neurons. Over time, this increase in levels of neurotransmitters—so important to regulating mood—helps to alleviate depression.

A main reason that MAOIs are not used often is because of their effects on another chemical called tyramine, which has a chemical structure similar to serotonin, dopamine, and norepinephrine.

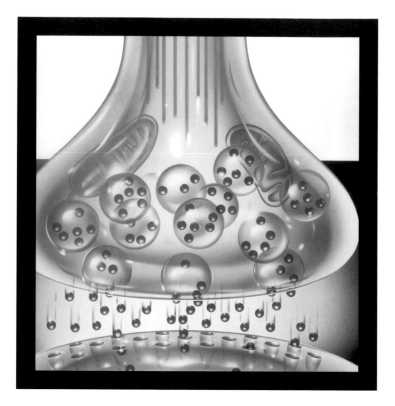

THIS IS WHAT A NERVE SYNAPSE LOOKS LIKE. WHEN NEUROTRANSMITTERS ARE RELEASED INTO A SYNAPSE, THEY HELP REGULATE MOOD.

Tyramine is not a neurotransmitter, nor does it play a role in the brain, but instead acts on the body's blood pressure system. If tyramine levels are too high, blood pressure rises dramatically. A rapid rise in blood pressure may put the person at risk for a heart attack, stroke, or other side effects of high blood pressure. Tyramine is found in high quantities in a number of different foods, including hard cheeses, red wine, chicken livers, avocados, eggplant, and aged and cured meat.

Like serotonin, dopamine, and norepinephrine, tyramine is degraded by monoamine oxidase. Taking an MAOI prevents this degradation, which raises the level not only of the neurotransmitters but also of tyramine. A serious side effect of taking an MAOI, therefore, is increase in tyramine that leads to high blood pressure.

Today, there are two types of MAOIs, the conventional type, called irreversible MAOIs, and the newer type, called reversible MAOIs or RMAOIs. The conventional MAOIS irreversibly inhibit monoamine oxidase. When their use is discontinued, the body requires two weeks before it can produce the natural enzyme again. The danger of severe, life-threatening high blood pressure limits the use of these drugs, and requires careful dietary and medication restrictions on patients taking them. The new MAOIs—as yet unavailable in the United States—are reversible in their inhibition of monoamine oxidase and thus have fewer side effects and restrictions.

The MAOI Experience
As is true for all antidepressants, MAOIs are not addictive, nor do they trigger feelings of elation or euphoria. MAOIs do not induce a "high" in those who take them. In fact, except for feeling an improvement in depressive symptoms that will probably occur within two to six weeks, people who take MAOIs are seldom aware of being on a medication.

However, all MAOIs may cause side effects, including restlessness, agitation, dizziness, dry mouth, sleep disturbances, and weight gain or loss. Constipation and other gastrointestinal disturbances may occur. Sweating and skin rashes have also been reported, as have sexual side effects, including loss of sex drive. Dangerously high blood pressure may occur and blood pressure also should be monitored. Despite these unpleasant side effects, MAOIs may be the only form of medication that alleviates depression in some people.

These side effects dissipate within a week or two. As discussed, these drugs also react with certain foods, as well as alcoholic beverages and other medications (including over-the-counter cold and allergy preparations, local anesthetics, amphetamines, antihistamines, insulin, narcotics, anti-Parkinson's disease medication, and some antidepressants, especially SSRIs). MAOIs can increase or enhance the action of SSRIs, causing a marked increase in their levels.

Indeed, when excessive serotonin stimulation occurs, a constellation of symptoms called "serotonin syndrome" may develop. The syndrome causes a patient to experience confusion, hallucinations, and ataxia, or the inability to coordinate voluntary muscular movements. Serotonin syndrome may be fatal if left untreated because of its effects on the circulatory system—it may cause heart attack or stroke.

Because of these potentially severe side effects and the need to restrict the diet to avoid tyramine-rich foods, MAOIs are rarely prescribed to either adults or teens. However, if someone with depression has been unable to tolerate or has failed to respond to other types of antidepressants, then MAOI treatment might be indicated. Treatment with MAOIs, as well as other antidepressants, requires careful monitoring by a physician.

Tricyclic Antidepressants (TCAs)

Prescribed since the 1950s, tricyclic antidepressants (TCAs) were among the first drugs developed to treat depression. They act to slow the reuptake of both serotonin and norepinephrine. Although quite effective in reducing symptoms of depression, TCAs also trigger a number of unpleasant, sometimes dangerous side effects. That's because the active substances in TCAs act not only on brain chemicals causing the depressive symptoms but also on the peripheral nervous system. Depending on dosage, TCAs may disrupt brain regions that control heart rate, appetite, muscle tension, and sexual function enough to outweigh their effects on mood.

The TCA Experience

TCAs do not cause elation or the feeling of being "high" in people who take them. In fact, after a few weeks when side effects tend to diminish, most people taking TCAs are unaware that they are on medication. People taking TCAs notice that their depressive symptoms diminish and they're able to function better. Usually, they are also able to sleep better and their appetites improve.

But the side effects of TCAs can be problematic for some people who take them. Interestingly, young people tend to experience fewer side effects than older people, although, again, the only antidepressant FDA-approved for use in adolescents is Prozac, an SSRI. However, doctors have prescribed these medications without FDA approval for many years. As is true for most other antidepressants, patients should avoid taking TCAs with other medications, including other antidepressants, especially MAOIs, without express advice from their doctors to do so.

Among the most common side effects of TCAs are feeling restless or anxious, having difficulty concentrating, and experiencing a host of physical symptoms such as dry mouth and eyes, constipation, drowsiness, appetite changes, nausea, and dizziness. There are some simple solutions to many of these side effects, such as chewing gum to alleviate dry mouth and using eye drops to moisten dry eyes. Eating a healthy diet, getting exercise, and drinking lots of water also helps people taking TCAs for depression better tolerate any side effects that emerge.

Because TCAs tend to slow the heart rate, which can cause irregular heartbeat, TCAs are generally not recommended for people with heart conditions. In addition, these drugs also can cause seizures in people with a history of seizures. The doctor may choose to prescribe a drug for such people, as well as for those who suffer unpleasant side effects that do not subside over a period of a few weeks or months.

Overdoses of TCAs can be life-threatening. In fact, overdoses of TCA are the leading cause of overdose deaths in the United States, and have been for at least a decade. Monitoring dosages and managing side effects are joint responsibilities of patients and their doctors. Patients should never lower or raise the amount of medication they take, or stop taking medication altogether, without first talking it over with the physician and following his or her advice.

Selective Serotonin Reuptake Inhibitors (SSRIs)
Although scientists are unsure of their exact mechanism, it appears that SSRIs work to relieve depression by selectively inhibiting the reuptake (reabsorption) of the neurotransmitter serotonin. By doing so, they allow more serotonin, one of the neurotransmitters known to boost mood, to stimulate the serotonin receptors in the brain. Over time, scientists believe that this stimulation leads to an increase in the amount of serotonin receptors. Another theory is that SSRIs actually trigger new neurons to grow in the area of the hippocampus, a region important for memory formation and mood.

The SSRIs, particularly fluoxetine (Prozac), are the most widely prescribed drugs in the world. While they have been heralded as wonder drugs because of their ability to alleviate symptoms of depression without causing debilitating side effects in most people who take them, concerns about their safety and effectiveness continue to be raised. Some users suffer from serious side effects, including weight gain, sexual dysfunction, and suicidal urges. Some experience a kind of emotional numbness, unable to feel joy or happiness. Some studies indicate that as many as 3 percent of those who have taken Prozac have increased suicidal urges.

Another complaint about Prozac and other SSRIs is that they are overprescribed, that doctors provide them to people who are experiencing not depression but merely a "case of the blues." Critics also believe that publicity over the effectiveness of the drugs has led many people to believe that there is a magic pill that will cure all of their problems and that working with a therapist to cope with psychological, social, and physical challenges is no longer necessary.

At the same time, as scientists continue to study these potentially serious side effects, millions of people who suffer from depression remain grateful for the drugs that allow them to feel and function better. It appears that, for the majority of patients, including teenagers, the benefits of Prozac and other similar antidepressants far outweigh the side effects. With proper medical supervision, these drugs can help countless people reclaim their lives from the ravages of depression.

Risk Factors and Warning Signs of Suicide

A constellation of influences—mental disorders, personality traits, genetic vulnerability, medical illness, psychosocial stressors—combine to undermine an individual's strength and will to live. Depression and alcoholism are underlying factors in more than two-thirds of all suicides. Other risk factors for suicide include:

- Being an adolescent;
- Having a history of prior suicide attempts;
- Experiencing a recent interpersonal loss, especially if already suffering from depression or substance abuse;
- Having feelings of low self-esteem and hopelessness;
- Having a family history of suicide in the last two generations.

Among the most common warning signs of suicide are:

- Extreme changes in behavior;
- A previous suicide attempt;
- Talk about death or suicide or "going away";
- Giving away favorite possessions.

SSRIs Prescribed to Treat Depression

Name of Drug	Fluoxetine
Brand Name	Prozac, Fotex, Serafam
Comments	FDA-approved for use in teens. Increases suicidal thoughts in about 1 of 50 people 18 years and younger, especially in the first few weeks of use. In rare cases, causes convulsions. Also used to treat anxiety disorders, eating disorders, and obsessive-compulsive disorder (OCD).
Name of Drug	Citolapram
Brand Name	Celexa, Cipramil
Comments	Not FDA-approved for use in teens. In rare cases, may cause suicidal thoughts or panic attacks, especially in the first few weeks of use. Also used to treat anxiety disorders.
Name of Drug	Escitalopram oxalate
Brand Name	Lexapro, Cipralex
Comments	In rare cases, causes mania and seizures. Never take with MAOIs. Also used to treat generalized anxiety disorder.
Name of Drug	Sertraline
Brand Name	Zoloft
Comments	Only approved for teenagers with OCD, not depression. Can trigger suicidal thoughts. Diarrhea, nausea, and vomiting may occur.
Name of Drug	Paroxetine
Brand Name	Paxil
Comments	Not FDA-approved for use in children or teens. Also used to treat OCD and panic disorders.

The SSRI Experience

As is true for other types of antidepressants, SSRIs do not act to make people who take them feel high. In fact, if someone is not depressed and takes one of these medications, chances are he or she will feel no mood changes at all. Those who are depressed, however, usually begin to feel symptoms of their disease dissipate within four to six weeks of starting treatment, or sometimes sooner. A sense of normality and a potential for happiness and optimism return.

As is true for all antidepressants, the most serious potential side effect is the risk of heightened thoughts of suicide. The FDA reports that about one in fifty people under the age of eighteen will experience thoughts of suicide when they take an SSRI. That's why it's important to report all signs that a teen is thinking of suicide to a physician as soon as possible, particularly if he or she is taking an antidepressant.

More typical and benign side effects of SSRIs include nervousness, headaches, and changes in sexual function. Weight gain or loss is common, as are gastrointestinal disturbances. Teeth grinding and insomnia (which affects up to about 14 percent of users) also are common. Usually side effects abate after a few weeks of use.

Unclassified Antidepressants

Following the success of Prozac, scientists continued to search for drugs that similarly targeted the brain's chemical imbalance without causing unpleasant side effects. A number of chemically unrelated drugs emerged from this research. Each one interacts differently with the neurotransmitters—serotonin and dopamine—that are tied to depression. One drug, venlafaxine (Effexor), for instance, acts as TCAs do by selectively inhibiting the reuptake of serotonin and norepinephrine. However, they do not attach to other neurotransmitter receptors and thus have far fewer side effects than the older antidepressant family. Bupropion (Wellbutrin), on the other hand, acts on the reuptake of serotonin and dopamine, causing unique effects and side effects for those who take it. Nefazodone (Serzone) blocks a specific serotonin subtype, while trazodone (Desyrel) targets serotonin.

The Newer Antidepressants

As is true with the other antidepressants, taking one of the unclassified antidepressants will not make a patient feel high or elated. It may take several weeks for their full effects to be felt and patience in finding the right drug at the right dose may be necessary. None of these drugs has been approved for use in treating depression in teens, but many doctors prescribe them off-label if treatment with Prozac does not reduce the symptoms, or if, for any reason, prescribing Prozac is contraindicated in a particular adolescent.

As a group, these unclassified antidepressants tend to have fewer and more tolerable side effects than their older counterparts. Some, such as

Wellbutrin, are known to reduce the incidence of sexual dysfunction that occurs with many SSRIs. On the other hand, some of these newer drugs appear to increase the number and incidence of seizures for those people who already suffer from seizure disorders.

The Future of Antidepressant Treatment for Teens
The number of teens being prescribed antidepressants—on- and off-label—increases every year. Without question, there remains a pressing need for more studies on how antidepressants work—or don't work—to relieve depression in the still-developing brains of children and adolescents. How these treatments compare to psychotherapy and how therapy and antidepressants work together to improve depression in teens is also a subject worthy of study. What we do know today is that untreated depression in teenagers remains the number one risk factor for suicide in this age group. When symptoms of depression develop, getting help from a qualified professional is the top priority for teens and their families.

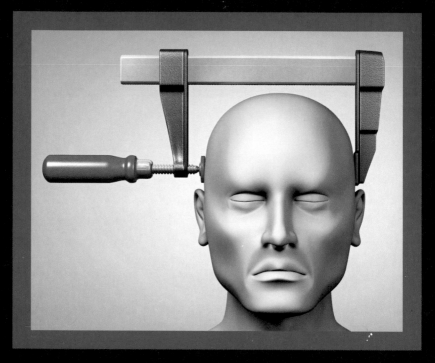

WHEN YOU HAVE A HEADACHE, IT CAN FEEL LIKE YOUR HEAD IS IN A VISE. ASPIRIN CAN SOMETIMES REDUCE THE SYMPTOMS, BUT IT DOESN'T GET TO THE ROOT OF WHAT CAUSED THE HEADACHE.

4 Taking Antidepressants

For the vast majority of depressed people— including teenagers—whose symptoms have not improved after undergoing therapy or other medical intervention, taking an antidepressant greatly improves their health and well-being. For those living with dysthymia (a milder form of depression), antidepressants can reignite a dormant spark of interest in living. For those with major depression, medication can literally save lives.

That said, it's important to point out that while antidepressant medication is effective for most people with depression, it is not a miracle cure. First, it fails to help improve depressive symptoms at all in some people; exactly how many people are resistant to drug therapy is unknown.

Second, anyone who develops depression is likely to have some issues in his or her personal life that need to be addressed with psychotherapy. Just as aspirin reduces a fever without clearing up the infection that causes it, antidepressants act by controlling symptoms but do not "cure" depression. Instead, they lessen the burden of symptoms and help make psychotherapy and other interventions more effective. Although antidepressants can dramatically change the way once-depressed people feel, other challenges they face will not suddenly disappear simply because they take medication. Depending on how severe and longstanding the depression has been, a teen recovering from the disorder may also suffer from low self-esteem and learned thought and behavior patterns to compensate for his or her depressed moods and low energy. That's another reason why combining drug therapy with counseling is so vital.

Another issue to consider is that—even today, more than halfway through the first decade of the twenty-first century—there remains a great deal of skepticism over, and even disdain for, psychotherapeutic drugs of any kind. For many of the same reasons that people—particularly teenagers—resist seeing a therapist (shame over needing help, worry that others will find out, doubt that such intervention will help), they also resist taking medication. Some feel special shame that their emotional problems require drug therapy. Others believe that even if medication makes you feel better, it doesn't really "count" because it isn't really "you." Others worry, usually needlessly, about unwanted side effects.

Deciding to Take an Antidepressant

Although antidepressants are usually quite safe, they are strong drugs that alter the workings of the brain and body, especially in teenagers, whose bodies and brains are still developing. Every person facing the decision to take this medication must consider the matter thoroughly, talking it over with both a therapist and the doctor who prescribes the medication, if the therapist is not authorized to pre-scribe medication.

Among the most important considerations is whether or not the patient is taking any other med-ications. Any medication—even an over-the-counter drug—has the potential to modify body chemistry and thus probably worsen an underlying health problem or create a new one. In addition, certain drugs may be dangerous when taken in combina-tion with one another or when taken with alcohol or, as in the case of MAOIs, with certain kinds of food. Before prescribing medication, the doctor should study a patient's medical history and check his or her current health status to make sure no existing medical condition would be adversely affected by antidepressant medication. It's the patient's responsibility—perhaps with the help of his or her parents—to tell the doctor about every medication used on a regular or occasional basis. This information will allow the doctor to prescribe the proper medication.

It is also important to let the doctor know of any problems with recreational drugs or alcohol. Such an issue is especially prominent among teens with

THESE TEENS ARE OUTSIDE OF A SCHOOL MAKING AN ILLEGAL DEAL TO BUY DRUGS. THE USE OF ILLEGAL DRUGS CAN BE VERY DANGEROUS—AND WILL DEFINITELY INTERFERE WITH THE EFFECT OF ANTIDEPRESSANT MEDICATIONS.

depression, who often self-medicate with alcohol or illegal drugs in an effort to relieve their depressive symptoms. If a teen with depression uses drugs or alcohol, he or she must get help for both the substance abuse problem and the depression. In fact, it is impossible to successfully treat one without dealing with the other. In one study of adults, 60 percent of people who had been admitted to an alcohol treatment program also suffered from depression, but only 10 percent had been treated for depression. In some cases, treatment in a substance abuse program may be necessary in order to "clear out" the remaining drugs or alcohol from the system before a patient could safely take an antidepressant.

Finally, many people, including teenagers, fear that by deciding to take an antidepressant, they are somehow giving control of their minds over to the drugs or to the doctor. Nothing could be further from the truth. By reestablishing the proper connections among the neurons in the brain, an antidepressant in effect hands the controls back to the person suffering from the disorder.

Unless a depressed teen is terribly ill and incapacitated, he or she will remain in charge of his or her recovery, whether or not medication is prescribed. Even after a teen decides, with input from parents, therapists, and physicians, to take medication, if ever he or she feels medication is no longer the right choice, the issue can be revisited among all involved.

Common Risks and Benefits of Antidepressants

Whether the benefits of taking an antidepressant outweigh the risks will vary from individual to individual. These are matters to be discussed with a physician. Some of the risks and benefits of taking antidepressants are:

BENEFITS	RISKS
1. Easy to prescribe, and is nonaddictive	1. Requires care of a physician
2. Proven to be very effective for most people	2. Requires ongoing counseling for those who take them
3. Few serious, long-term side effects occur	3. Side effects, some serious, can occur in some people
4. Can be lifesaving for people with severe depression	4. May trigger dangerous mood disorders, mood swings, or even suicidal thoughts in rare cases
5. Medication is easy to take, usually	5. Medication must be taken on a one-dose-a-day schedule and other drugs and alcohol must be avoided

Choosing an Antidepressant

At this writing in 2006, fluoxetine (Prozac) is the only antidepressant approved by the federal Food and Drug Administration (FDA) for use by young people under the age of eighteen. What the designation means is that the FDA feels that enough studies have been performed to conclude that Prozac is safe for teenagers to take. Even this antidepressant contains a warning about the heightened risk of suicide and other negative side effects in this age group. The FDA cautions that this medication requires careful, constant monitoring by a physician in combination with therapy.

In addition to Prozac, there are more than two dozen other types of drugs used to treat depression and other mood disorders that physicians may—and often do—prescribe to teens off-label. Although the FDA will not approve the other drugs without more studies, the American Academy of Child and Adolescent Psychiatry believes that Prozac and other antidepressants—SSRIs in particular—have benefits for depressed adolescents that far outweigh their risks, as long as young patients receive careful monitoring combined with psychotherapy.

Which drug or combination of drugs works for any given individual depends largely upon his or her own particular brain chemistry and constellation of symptoms. Some people may respond better to one medication than another. Since no test exists to measure exactly how one's brain chemistry is imbalanced or why it became that way, prescribing an antidepressant is often a hit-or-miss affair.

"I didn't even really know that I was depressed," recalls Bill, now a twenty-two-year-old college graduate. "I was angry. That was my main emotion—anger, and maybe irritation, edginess. I also couldn't get out of bed and I was eating so much I was gaining weight."

When Bill was seventeen, he started to see a therapist at a school counselor's suggestion. For several weeks, the therapist and Bill worked through some of the problems he was having with school, friends, and family. "By talking through some of this stuff, I realized—slowly—how sad I felt. It wasn't anger, it was hopelessness, and a little self-hatred. For two or three weeks, I would cry and cry at my therapist appointments, even as things with school and my family started to get better. That's when he thought maybe an antidepressant would help."

Bill and his therapist talked the matter over with Bill's parents and his regular doctor. Together, they decided to start Bill on Prozac. "It didn't work, not even after a month. It didn't make me crazy or anything, but I kept feeling as if a great weight was on me. It made me edgy and nervous, and instead of sleeping all the time, I had trouble sleeping at all."

Because Bill's symptoms didn't improve, Bill's therapist and doctor decided to switch him to another SSRI, Lexapro. "That one worked, and it worked kind of quickly. I stopped taking all medication for a couple of weeks, then started Lexapro. Within a few weeks, I felt better. It didn't change my life, but soon things seemed much more manageable. I could handle my life without so much struggling. I didn't have any side effects at all that I recognized. I took it for about two years, maybe three. So far, I haven't needed it again, but I'd certainly do it again rather than feel the way I did before I took it."

That said, it is likely that a physician who decides a teenager suffering from depression would benefit from the use of an antidepressant along with psychotherapy will probably start by prescribing Prozac, along with continuing therapy. The dosage prescribed will depend on the individual patient and his or her age, weight, and body chemistry, among other factors. Because it may take up to two months for an antidepressant to take effect, doctors will monitor the effects and side effects of these drugs very carefully during this period. It's important that anyone taking an antidepressant be as patient and flexible as possible, and not stop taking medication because of minor side effects. Antidepressants attempt to reestablish a proper balance of neurotransmitters in the brain, which can be a pretty tricky enterprise that often requires a bit of finesse on the part of the doctor and a great deal of patience on the part of the teen taking the drug.

Once the doctor prescribes the medication, the patient becomes responsible for taking the drug and understanding what to expect from it. Here are some of the questions every patient should ask before beginning treatment with an antidepressant:

- What is the name of the medication and how does it work?
- How and when do I take it?
- What foods, drinks, and other medications or activities should I avoid while taking this medication?

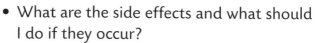

- What are the side effects and what should I do if they occur?
- Under what circumstances should I go to an emergency room when side effects occur?
- What should I do if I forget to take my medicine?
- How will I know if the medicine is working?
- Is there any risk that I could become addicted?
- Can you provide me with any written information about the medication that I can keep with me?
- Under what circumstances should I stop taking the medication?

Managing Antidepressants

Remaining under a doctor's care is extremely important for teens (and adults) who choose to take an antidepressant. In addition to continuing counseling sessions with a psychotherapist, teenagers taking antidepressants should visit the medical doctor who prescribed the drug:

- Once a week for four weeks;
- Every two weeks for the next month;
- At the end of their twelfth week taking the drug;
- More often if problems or questions arise.

Most people who take antidepressants find the process relatively easy and problem-free, especially after the first few weeks when the drugs "kick in" to improve symptoms and most side effects. As discussed, most people don't feel much of a change in their mood for at least two to four weeks, sometimes longer. If the doctor believes that a sufficient time on the drug has passed and a patient's symptoms have not improved, the doctor can decide to (1) change the dosage, (2) try a different drug in the same class of antidepressants, (3) switch to a drug in a different class, or (4) try a combination of medications. If the doctor decides to change the dose or the type of medication, it might take another few weeks for improvement to occur, and even longer before the medication's full impact is felt.

A study in the March 23, 2006, issue of the *New England Journal of Medicine* found that one in three depressed patients who previously did not improve using an antidepressant became symptom-free with the help of an additional medication, and one in four became symptom-free after switching to a different antidepressant.

If the patient feels only a little better on a particular medication, the doctor may decide to augment the therapy with the addition of another type of drug, such as thyroid medication or stimulants. A short course of stimulants, for instance, may help improve stubborn symptoms of fatigue and listlessness. In some cases, if the doctor and patient decide to switch to another medication, a transition phase, typically known as a "wash-out period," may be required in order to get one drug out of the system before introducing another. When switching between an MAOI and a TCA or SSRI, doctors usually recommend at least a two-week wait depending on the drug chosen. Sometimes, it may take three or more tries on different drugs or combinations of drugs to achieve the right balance.

The important thing is not to get discouraged. Many people need to try a few different dosages, even a few different drugs, before hitting the right solution. Fortunately, statistics show that more than 65 percent of people who do not respond to one type of drug will improve on another. One reason why the FDA continues to study the effects of the wide range of antidepressants on adolescents and children is so that, in the future, doctors will have more FDA-approved medications to choose from when treating young people with depression who do not respond to therapy alone.

While taking antidepressants, it's important to follow all of the doctor's instructions and warnings. Most doctors strongly discourage using alcohol while using antidepressants, especially for teens. Not only does alcohol depress the central nervous system, but it stimulates enzymes that break down the medication, lowering the amount in the blood and thus making it more difficult to maintain therapeutic levels. Alcohol also tends to enhance the sedating effects of antidepressants that cause drowsiness as an initial side effect. Some other general rules to follow include:

- Never increase or decrease a medication's dose without first consulting the doctor.
- Never share medication with someone else, even someone the same age who appears to suffer from similar symptoms.
- Make a chart of when medication is taken and when, if ever, side effects occur.

Although side effects with Prozac and other newer antidepressants tend to be mild and usually subside within a few weeks, teens who take these drugs should report all side effects as soon as possible to their doctors. Among the most urgent side effects to report right away, by the patient or by family members or friends who notice them, include:

- New or more thoughts of suicide;
- Trying to commit suicide;
- New or worse depression;
- New or worse anxiety;
- Feeling very agitated or restless;
- Panic attacks;
- Difficulty sleeping;
- Acting aggressive or violent;
- Impulsivity;
- Hyperactivity;
- Other unusual changes in behavior.

As discussed, how long a person takes an antide-pressant varies. As a general rule, once someone has been symptom-free for about six months, he or she can—working with the doctor—taper off the med-ication, while carefully watching for the recurrence of symptoms.

Other Uses for Antidepressants

Because of the way antidepressants work to rebal-ance brain chemistry, they have proven to be useful in treating other mental and physical illnesses as well, including chronic pain, attention deficit/ hyperactivity disorder (ADHD), and obsessive-compulsive disorder, among others.

Chronic Pain

Chronic pain is one of the most common conditions in the United States. A poll conducted by ABC News in May 2005 noted that about 40 percent of all Americans suffer pain on a regular basis. In addition to traditional over-the-counter medications, doc-tors frequently prescribe antidepressants to help their patients with chronic pain.

Tricyclic antidepressants seem to work best for the burning or searing pain common after nerve damage, which sometimes occurs with diabetes, shingles, and strokes. These drugs are also effective in some people as a preventive medication for migraines and for fibromyalgia, a common and painful arthritis-related condition that causes chronic muscle pain.

MORE AMERICANS SUFFER FROM CHRONIC BACK PAIN THAN ALMOST ANY OTHER CHRONIC ILLNESS. IN SOME CASES, ANTIDEPRESSANTS HAVE PROVEN TO BE EFFECTIVE COUNTERS TO PAIN.

While the FDA has yet to approve the use of tricyclic antidepressants in pain management, often doctors prescribe them to treat many chronic pain conditions even when depression is not a factor. Amitriptyline, known by its brand name Elavil, is the tricyclic antidepressant most commonly prescribed for pain, and it is the one that has been studied most thoroughly. Other tricyclic antidepressants used for pain include the following:

- Imipramine (Tofranil)
- Nortriptyline (Pamelor)
- Desipramine (Norpram)

Why these medications work to alleviate pain is still not fully understood. They may increase neuro-transmitters in the spinal cord that reduce pain signals. As is true for their use to relieve depression, however, they don't work immediately to relieve pain.

Attention Deficit Hyperactivity Disorder (ADHD)
One of the most common behavioral disorders suffered by children and adolescents in the United States today, ADHD affects at least four million young people, and about a third of those people continue to suffer from the disease as adults. People with ADHD are easily distracted, hyperactive, and often very impulsive.

The first-line treatment for ADHD is the use of stimulants, including Ritalin, Cylert, and Concerta, among others. In those children and adults who do not respond to stimulants, or who cannot tolerate their side effects, antidepressants often offer the next-best solution. Although fluoxetine (Prozac) is commonly used, it is the tricyclic antidepressants that seem to work best for ADHD, especially for treating hyperactivity and inattentiveness.

Obsessive-Compulsive Disorder
Obsessive-compulsive disorder (OCD) is a potentially disabling anxiety disorder. A person with OCD suffers from intrusive and unwanted thoughts and repeatedly performs tasks to get rid of the thoughts. For example, someone with OCD may

fear that everything he or she touches is contaminated with germs, and in order to ease that fear, he or she repeatedly washes his or her hands.

Tricyclic antidepressants rarely work to relieve the symptoms of OCD. Instead, SSRIs seem to rebalance brain chemistry in people who suffer from this condition. Clomipramine (Anafranil), which is an SSRI, has been used to treat OCD for decades. In addition to clomipramine, several other SSRIs have been shown effective in treating OCD, including fluvoxamine (Luvox), fluoxetine (Prozac), sertraline (Zoloft) and paroxetine (Paxil).

As is true for a depressed person who takes antidepressants, those who use them to treat these and other health conditions must work closely with a physician, keep track of and report all side effects, and be patient with the ups and downs of treatment.

MEDICATION ALONE IS NOT THE MOST EFFECTIVE WAY TO
TREAT DEPRESSION. A COMBINATION OF MEDICATION AND
COUNSELING—SOMETIMES INDIVIDUAL, SOMETIMES GROUP,
AS SHOWN HERE—IS RECOMMENDED AS THE BEST WAY TO
GET BETTER.

5 Complements to Antidepressants

Antidepressants appear to be safe and helpful treatments for depression in both teenagers and adults, if properly administered and monitored. However, medication is not the only answer to the problem of depression and related disorders. In fact, the American Psychiatric Society recommends that all adolescents who take antidepressants also undergo counseling.

In addition, there are several alternatives to medication that may alleviate symptoms of depression. As long as teens remain under the care of a physician who monitors their progress, using such alternatives—in combination with talk therapy—may be a safer option for those with milder forms of depression, or for those people for whom medication does not work.

Let's Talk About It

Past mistakes, current complications, future goals: for many teens, especially those coping with depression, psychotherapy helps put these issues into proper perspective. Although there are many types of talk therapy, they all have the same ultimate goal: to help people suffering with depression reestablish connections with their full range of emotions—joy as well as sadness, pride as well as shame and guilt, strength as well as fear, anticipation as well as disappointment—within the safety of a trained therapist's office. Therapy also helps people change their behavior so that they make better choices in the ways they act and react to the world around them.

Among the many goals of therapy the first is to simply feel better. Sometimes, just going to a therapist helps those with depression feel as if they've gained some control over their situations. Other strategies include eating better and getting more exercise. These keys to well-being contribute more than most people realize to the state of mental health.

As people with depression begin to feel better, either through medication or therapy, or both, they are then able to look at what may have triggered the disorder to begin with. Perhaps a divorce or death of a loved one or a move from a familiar neighborhood to a new environment triggered the descent. Even the people who experience them do not recognize the factors that cause their depression, which is why the objective help of a therapist can be so useful. A therapist also helps people with depression objectively assess what in their lives needs fixing and what is more on track than they realize.

Choosing a Therapist
There are many different types of professionals who are trained to treat depression in teens and adults. Medical doctors, such as pediatricians or general practitioners, are able to prescribe antidepressants, but they usually do not have the time, inclination, or training to counsel their patients on a regular basis. Psychiatrists, psychologists, social workers, and therapists are all qualified to help teens fight their way through to the other side of depression.

- Psychiatrists are medical doctors who specialize in the diagnosis and treatment of psychological disorders. They have completed medical school, a year-long internship, and a three-year residency program that provides training in diagnosis and treatment of psychiatric disorders. They can prescribe medications and make medical decisions.
- Psychologists have completed a graduate program in human psychology that includes clinical training and internships in counseling, psychotherapy, or psychological training. Although most have a doctoral

degree (either a Ph.D. or a Psy.D.), psychologists have not studied medicine nor can they prescribe medication. Most states require that psychologists be licensed in order to practice independently.

- Certified social workers (C.S.W.s) or licensed clinical social workers (L.C.S.W.s) have completed a two-year graduate program with specialized training in helping people with mental problems, in addition to conventional social work. Most states certify or license social workers and require the passage of a qualifying exam.

Probably the best way for people to choose among the therapists available to treat depression in the area is to get advice from their primary care physicians. Other sources include local medical or psychiatric societies, community health centers, and medical schools. Another factor to consider is insurance: teens will want to check with their parents to see what kind of coverage for psychological counseling their health insurance provides and who among those professionals in the area accepts that insurance.

Finding the right therapist may not happen on the first try or even the second. Although a therapist is not a friend, it is important that all patients feel comfortable and safe with their therapists. That may be difficult for most teens, who most likely will resist the process altogether at first. But only by having a trusting relationship—called the therapeutic alliance—with accepting and supportive professionals will patients be able to reveal their innermost feelings.

Types of Therapy

Most mental health professionals are trained in a variety of psychotherapeutic techniques.

They will tailor their approaches to the needs of each patient's personality and needs. During the first few appointments, therapists make careful assessments of new patients' current problems, psychological and medical history, and family history. Only then will they choose a particular approach. Among those available are:

- *Psychodynamic psychotherapy.* Psychodynamic therapy is based on the premise that current difficulties are the result of unresolved past conflicts. By bringing these conflicts into present awareness, the patient can understand and deal with them in a more appropriate manner. The therapist will act as a guide to building self-awareness and understanding.
- *Behavioral therapy.* As its names implies, behavioral therapy concentrates on identifying and changing negative patterns of behavior. This type of therapy is especially helpful for disorders characterized by

SOMETIMES, PEOPLE BECOME SO OBSESSED WITH WEIGHT THAT THEY ACTUALLY SPEND TIME MEASURING THEIR THIGHS. THIS CAN LEAD TO EATING DISORDERS AND DEPRESSION. THERAPY CAN HELP WITH THESE PROBLEMS.

specific abnormal ways of acting, such as substance abuse, alcoholism, or eating disorders. Since so many teens with depression also suffer from such disorders, behavioral therapy may be an effective treatment for teens. The therapist often will provide "homework assignments"—specific tasks that must be accomplished by the next session.

- *Cognitive behavioral therapy (CBT).* This type of therapy recognizes that emotional health is related to thought patterns and beliefs about the world. In this view, self-criticism and negative thinking patterns can trigger depression, and this is especially true for teens. In fact, CBT is among the most successful types of therapy for adolescents because it addresses negative thought patterns common to this age group. At this time, people tend to constantly berate themselves, expecting themselves to fail, and making negative, usually inaccurate, assessments of what others think of them. Cognitive behavioral therapy works to reframe negative thought patterns, to change them into realistic and reaffirming ones. Among the dysfunctional thinking patterns addressed are all-or-nothing thinking ("If I gain two pounds, I'm a fat slob."), and magnifying or minimizing ("If I stub my toe in the morning, my whole day will be awful"). Cognitive behavioral therapy is relatively brief (usually between sixteen and twenty sessions) and works to address a patient's most pressing concerns.
- *Interpersonal psychotherapy (IPT).* This type

of therapy is based on the theory that disturbed social and personal relationships, especially among family members, can cause or precipitate depression. The therapist helps the patient understand how depression and interpersonal conflicts are related. This type of therapy appears to be helpful for young people. Like CBT, it is usually short-term, consisting of about twelve to sixteen weekly sessions.

- *Group therapy.* Both cognitive and interpersonal therapy can take place in individual sessions or in a group setting. For teens resistant to therapy, and who do so only at the insistence of their parents and doctors, a group setting may be a good compromise. Young people tend to find group sessions less threatening. It's easier for them to learn social skills in a more relaxed, less stigmatizing environment. This is especially true of those also suffering with a substance abuse problem or eating disorder.

No matter what type of therapy is chosen, every young patient who takes antidepressants must complement that treatment with a form of therapy. Recent studies prove that the combination of therapy and medication is the surest way for teens to find relief from this potentially debilitating disease.

Living Well

The clichés are endless: "You are what you eat." "A healthy body is a healthy mind." In this instance, however, the clichés have merit. Study after study shows that eating well, exercising often, and getting enough sleep help prevent depressive episodes and alleviate depressive symptoms when they do occur.

- *Sleep well.* Sleep problems are often the first and most serious symptoms of depression and teens are especially susceptible.
- *Enjoy a healthy diet.* Food is not only nourishment that provides the body with the raw materials it needs to function. It should also be a source of pleasure. Unfortunately, too many people, especially young women, are so afraid of food—of its calories and fat content particularly—that they've lost the ability to enjoy cooking, eating, and sharing meals with others.
- *Avoid alcohol.* Teens prone to depression all too often self-medicate with alcohol—a counterproductive strategy—since alcohol acts as a depressant on the central nervous system. It's especially important to avoid alcohol while taking any medication, including antidepressants.
- *Exercise.* The benefits of physical activity are almost too many to mention. When it comes to mental health, exercise allows

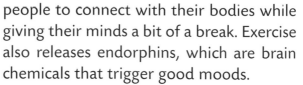

people to connect with their bodies while giving their minds a bit of a break. Exercise also releases endorphins, which are brain chemicals that trigger good moods.
- *Reduce stress.* Stress is a fact of life for teenagers today and it's a special burden for those who also suffer from depression. Exercise helps relieve stress, as do techniques such as biofeedback and meditation.

Natural Alternatives to Antidepressants
In the last two decades or so, there has been a remarkable explosion in the kinds and numbers of herbal remedies and other so-called natural medicines available to treat a host of conditions, including depression and other mood disorders. This influx has come from a greater understanding and appreciation of other forms of healing, some of which come from Eastern countries with far older traditions. Many focus on taking natural substances that tend not to be as processed or as strong as modern Western medicines.

It should be noted, however, that just because a substance is labeled "natural" doesn't make it either safe or effective. The FDA regulates dietary supplements under a different set of regulations than those covering "conventional" foods and prescription and over-the-counter drug products. Unlike the rigorous testing and approval regimen that medicines must undergo, the production and sale of herbal remedies receive much less oversight.

Under the Dietary Supplement Health and Education Act of 1994 (DSHEA), the dietary supplement manufacturer—not an objective government agency—is responsible for ensuring that a dietary supplement is safe before it is marketed. The FDA is responsible for taking action against any unsafe dietary supplement product only after it reaches the market. Generally, manufacturers do not need to register their products with the FDA nor get FDA approval before producing or selling dietary supplements. The FDA's post-marketing responsibilities include: monitoring safety, e.g., voluntary dietary supplement adverse event reporting; product information, such as labeling, claims, package inserts, and accompanying literature. The Federal Trade Commission regulates dietary supplement advertising.

Because of the significant risk of buying and using products that either are not effective treatments or actually can do harm, the federal government's National Institutes of Health Office of Alternative Medicine recommends the following before getting involved in any alternative therapy, including over-the-counter herbal remedies described in this chapter:

- Discuss all treatments with your primary care provider, who needs this information in order to have a complete picture of your treatment plan.

- Obtain objective information about the therapy. Read as much as you can about the substance or treatment, talk it over further with the your doctor, and ask about the advantages and disadvantages, risks, side effects, costs, results, and over what time span results can be expected.
- Consider the costs. Alternative treatments and medicines may not be reimbursable by health insurance.

That said, there are a number of herbal remedies that appear to benefit people who suffer from mild forms of depression. They should never be taken instead of a medicine prescribed by a doctor nor in addition to the medicine unless discussed with the physician beforehand. NEVER stop taking an antidepressant without a doctor's permission, even if you intend to start taking an alternative substance.

St. John's Wort
St. John's wort (*Hypericum perforatum* in Latin) is a long-lived plant with yellow flowers. The compounds hypericin and hyperforin produce the herb's primary physical and psychological effects. As is true for mainstream antidepressants, scientists are unsure of how these compounds actually work in the body. Preliminary studies suggest that St. John's wort might work in a way similar to SSRIs by preventing nerve cells in the brain from reabsorbing

THE HERB ST. JOHN'S WORT IS USED BY MANY AS A NATURAL TREATMENT FOR DEPRESSION. IT WORKS BEST FOR MILD DEPRESSION, BUT, AS WITH PRESCRIPTION ANTIDEPRESSANTS, IT CAN ALSO HAVE SIDE EFFECTS.

the chemical messenger serotonin. Another theory is that they reduce levels of a protein involved in the body's immune system functioning.

The results of modern studies are mixed when it comes to determining how successful St. John's wort is at alleviating symptoms of depression. In Europe, results from a number of scientific studies have supported the effectiveness of certain St. John's wort extracts for depression. An overview of twenty-three clinical studies involving more than 1,700 patients found that the herb might be useful in cases of mild to moderate depression. The studies, published in a 1996 issue of the *British Medical*

Journal, reported that St. John's wort was more effective than a placebo (sugar pill) and appeared to produce fewer side effects than some standard antidepressants. In 2001, however, a study published in the *Journal of the American Medical Association*, funded by the pharmaceutical company Pfizer, Inc., found that St. John's wort was not effective for treating major depression. But another study, published in the *American Journal of Psychiatry* in 2002, found that a St. John's wort extract was found to be safe and more effective than treatment with a placebo. More studies are under way today that may clarify the matter further.

St. John's wort can cause side effects. Research from the National Institutes of Health has shown that St. John's wort interacts badly with some drugs, including antidepressants, as well as with chemotherapeutic, or anticancer, drugs, and with medications that help prevent the body from rejecting transplanted organs (such as cyclosporine). Using St. John's wort limits these drugs' effectiveness. People also can experience side effects from taking St. John's wort. The most common side effects include dry mouth, dizziness, diarrhea, nausea, increased sensitivity to sunlight, and fatigue.

Ginkgo Biloba

The ginkgo biloba tree is considered to be the oldest living species of tree. It can be traced back more than two hundred million years, existing even before the Ice Age. Each tree may live as long as a

THE GINGKO TREE IS THE OLDEST SPECIES OF TREE. ITS SEEDS AND LEAVES HAVE
BEEN USED TO CURE AILMENTS AND LIFT MOODS FOR CENTURIES.

thousand years and does not bear flowers until it is twenty to thirty years old. Chinese medicine has used the seeds and leaves of the ginkgo tree to treat a variety of ailments for centuries.

In Europe, where it is widely heralded as a mental and vascular stimulant, ginkgo sales account for more than one percent of all alternative medicine purchases. In Germany and France it is the most frequently prescribed herbal medicine and is in the top five of all medical prescriptions written in those countries. Recently, physicians in the United States have begun to recognize the wealth of medicinal uses for this natural remedy.

Ginkgo is known to improve blood flow to the brain, which may help explain why some people who take it find that their memories improve and their moods lift. One review of eight controlled studies found it to improve memory loss, depressed mood, anxiety, and difficulties with concentration. It seems to be especially helpful in treating symptoms of mild depression in the elderly.

Side effects of gingko tend to be very slight and include headache, indigestion, and allergic skin reactions. It is unknown at this time exactly how the use of ginkgo interacts with other medication. Teens with depression should only use this supplement if they have permission from their doctors.

SAM-e

SAM-e is another natural antidepressant that studies show may help improve symptoms of depression. It's full name is s-adenosylmethionine, a substance—called an amino acid—that is found in every cell but whose function is not clearly understood. It causes several metabolic reactions in cells and helps maintain neuronal membrane function, which is probably why it appears to help relieve depression.

SAM-e has only been available since 1999 and has not been approved by the FDA for use in treating depression. As is true of all other alternative medications, a doctor's permission is necessary before anyone with depression—especially someone already taking a prescription medicine—takes SAM-e to treat their symptoms.

GLOSSARY

acetylcholine—A neurotransmitter that helps to regulate memory. It is also one of the principal neurotransmitters involved in bodily functions that are automatic, such as sweating and heart rate.

addiction—A pattern of behavior based on great physical and/or psychological need for a substance or activity. Addiction is characterized by compulsion, loss of control, and continued repetition of behavior regardless of the consequences.

anorexia nervosa—A chronic, sometimes fatal eating disorder involving loss of appetite or inability to eat that results in malnutrition, severe weight loss, and medical complications. Anorexia is frequently associated with depression.

anxiety disorder—Any of several psychological disorders characterized by inappropriate and excessive physical and emotional symptoms of anxiety, such as restlessness, rapid heartbeat and respiration, and fear. Agoraphobia, obsessive-compulsive disorder, post-traumatic stress disorder, and generalized anxiety disorder are among the most common. Anxiety disorders are frequently associated with depression.

attention deficit hyperactivity disorder—A mental disorder characterized by limited attention span, restlessness, distractability, hyperactivity, and impulsiveness.

behavior modification—A type of psychotherapy that attempts to change behavior by rewarding a desired behavior and punishing unwanted behavior; substituting a new response to a given stimulus.

bipolar disorder—A mood disorder characterized by recurrent, alternating episodes of depression and mania. Formerly called manic depression.

chronobiology—The study of internal body rhythms in order to map hormonal, nerve, and immune system cyclical functions. Some scientists believe that a disruption of normal body rhythms lies at the heart of depression.

cognitive therapy—A therapeutic approach that considers depression to be the result of pessimistic ways of thinking and distorted attitudes about oneself and one's life. The patient is able to relieve depression by learning new ways to think about his or her situation through role playing, discussion, and assigned tasks.

cortisol—A hormone produced by the body's adrenal glands, which are located above the kidneys. Cortisol is secreted in large amounts during times of stress and also on a cyclical basis according to internal sleep-wake rhythms.

dopamine—One of the neurotransmitters that may play a role in depression.

dysthymia—A chronic depressive state that lasts at least two years with symptoms more mild (but generally longer lasting) than major depression. Symptoms include feelings of inadequacy, hopelessness, low energy, and an inability to enjoy pleasurable activities.

endocrine disorder—The network of tissues and glands that produce hormones and secrete them into the blood for transport to target organs. Disorders of the endocrine system often cause depressive symptoms.

endorphins—Chemicals that help to elevate mood and alleviate pain. Low levels of endorphins are related to depression.

epinephrine—Also called adrenaline, a substance produced by the adrenal gland, often in response to stress. It is responsible for many of the physical manifestations of fear and anxiety.

hormones—Substances secreted by the endocrine system that have specific effects on organs and processes. Hormones are often referred to as "chemical messengers," and influence such diverse activities as growth, sexual development, metabolism, and sleep cycles.

L-tryptophan—The major building block of the neurotransmitter serotonin.

monoamine oxidase inhibitors (MAOIs)—Antidepressant medication that works by inhibiting monoamine oxidase, an enzyme that breaks down norepinephrine, serotonin, dopamine, and other neurotransmitters.

narcotic—Any drug that is derived from or has a chemical structure similar to that of an opiate and which relieves pain and alters mood. Most narcotics are addictive.

neurons—Nerve cells, the basic units of the nervous system. Neurons are able to conduct impulses and communicate by releasing and receiving neurotransmitters.

neurotransmitters—Chemicals that result in the sending of nerve signals, including serotonin, dopamine, and norepinephrine. Neurotransmitters are released by neurons. When an imbalance among them occurs, emotional and physical symptoms result.

norepinephrine—A neurotransmitter thought to be involved in affective disorders like depression.

psychotherapy—Treatment of psychiatric disorders involving support, reassurance, and reeducation of the patient.

receptors—Specialized molecules on the surface of neurons to which particular neurotransmitters attach after their release from another neurotransmitter. This binding allows a message to be passed from one neuron to another.

selective serotonin reuptake inhibitor (SSRI)— A type of antidepressant that works to prevent the reuptake of the neurotransmitter serotonin. This allows messages about emotion and behavior to be sent and received more efficiently.

serotonin—A neurotransmitter found in the brain and the body involved in behavior, emotion, and appetite.

synapse—The gap between the nerve endings of two neurons. For a message to pass across the synapse, it needs help from a neurotransmitter.

tricyclic antidepressants—Any of several drugs used to treat depression that have a three-ring chain as part of their chemical structure.

FURTHER INFORMATION

Books

Cefrey, Holly. *Antidepressants*. New York: The Rosen Group, 2000.

Cobain, Bev. *When Nothing Matters Anymore: A Survival Guide for Depressed Teens*. Minneapolis, MN: Free Spirit Publications, 1998.

Mitchell, E. Siobhan. *Antidepressants.* Philadelphia: Chelsea House, 2004.

Organizations

National Alliance for the Mentally Ill (NAMI)
2107 Wilson Boulevard, Suite 300
Arlington, VA 22201

1-800-950-NAMI
www.nami.org

National Institute of Mental Health
6001 Executive Boulevard
Rockville, MD 20892
www.nimh.nih.gov

International Foundation for Depressive Illness (IFred)
7040 Bembe Beach Road
Annapolis, MD 21403
1-410-268-0044
www.ifred.org

Internet Mental Health
www.mentalhealth.com

Substance Abuse and Mental Health Services Administration
www.mentalhealth.samhsa.gov

BIBLIOGRAPHY

Books

Appleton, William S. *The New Antidepressants and Antianxieties*. New York: The Penguin Group, 2004.

Barondes, Samuel H. *Mood Genes: Hunting for the Origins of Mania and Depression*. New York: Oxford University Press, 1999.

Glenmullen, J. *Prozac Backlash: Overcoming the Dangers of Prozac, Zoloft, Paxil, and Other Antidepressants*. New York: Touchstone, 2001.

Koplewicz, H. S. *More than Moody: Recognizing and Treating Adolescent Depression*. New York: Putnam Publishing Group, 2002.

Mondimore, Francis Mark. *Adolescent Depression: A Guide for Parents*. Baltimore: John Hopkins Press, 2002.

Monitoring the Future Study: A Continuing Study of American Youth. *Overview of Key Findings, 2005*.

Journal Articles

Beers, S. U., and M. DeBello, "Neuropsychology and function in children with maltreatment-related post-traumatic stress disorder." *American Journal of Psychiatry* 2002, 159: 483–486.

Dahl, R. E., and D. S. Lewin, "Pathways to adolescent health, sleep regulation and behavior." *Journal of Adolescent Health* 2002, 31: 175–184.

Ma, J., and K. U. Lee, "Depression treatment during outpatient visits by U.S. children and adolescents." *Journal of Adolescent Health* 2005, 37: 434–442.

March, J., and S. Silvas, et. al., "Fluoxetine, cognitive-behavorial therapy for adolescents with depression. Treatment for Adolescents with Depression Study (TADS)." *Journal of the American Medical Association* 2004, 297: 807–820.

Swan, A. C., "What is bipolar disorder?" *American Journal of Psychiatry*, 2006. 163: 177–179.

Weiss, Jeffrey, "Antidepressant adherence and suicide risk in depressed youth." *American Journal of Psychiatry*, 2003. 162: 1756–1757.

INDEX

ABOUT THE AUTHOR

Suzanne LeVert is the author of about thirty young adult and adult nonfiction books. She specializes in health and medical subjects. LeVert has, most recently, written *Nicotine* in the Drugs series. Born in Natick, Massachusetts, LeVert practices law in Virginia.